THE MAYOR'S OFFICE

David and Patricia Armentrout

Rourke
Publishing LLC
Vero Beach, Florida 32964

www.rourkepublishing.com

PHOTO CREDITS: © sgursozlu: Title Page; © paulaphoto: page 4; © Cary Kalscheuer: page 5; © Gregory James Van Raalte: page 6; © Jacob Wackerhausen: page 7; © Wendell Franks: page 8; © Benjamin F. Haith: page 9 left; © Valerie Loiseleux: page 9 right; ©Armentrout: page 10; © Marvin Nauman: page 11, 16; © JOHN HUGHEL, JR: page 13; © Anton Foltin: page 14; ©Philip H. Eckerberg: page 15; © Alan C. Heison: page 17; © U.S. airforce: page 18; © Andrew F. Kazmierski: page 19; © David Gilder: page 20; © R. D. Ward: page 21; © George Armstrong: page 22;

Edited by

Cover design by Teri Intzegian
Interior design by Teri Intzegian

Library of Congress Cataloging-in-Publication Data

Armentrout, David, 1962-
  The mayor's office / David and Patricia Armentrout.
    p. cm. -- (Our community)
  ISBN 978-1-60472-338-0
  1. Mayors--Juvenile literature. I. Armentrout, Patricia, 1960- II. Title.
  JS141.A76 2009
  352.23'216--dc22

                    2008016346

Printed in the USA

CG/CG

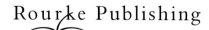

Rourke Publishing

www.rourkepublishing.com – rourke@rourkepublishing.com
Post Office Box 3328, Vero Beach, FL 32964

Table of Contents

Leadership

What makes a community a good place to live? Is it safe? Are there places to work? Does it have good schools and parks? It takes leadership to make a community strong.

Good leaders know how important schools are to the community.

Local **governments** run cities and towns. A mayor is a government leader. Does your community have a mayor?

A mayor works for the people who live in the community.

Let's take a Vote

In many cities, people elect mayors. This means **citizens** vote for, or choose them to serve.

Citizens have the right and duty to vote.

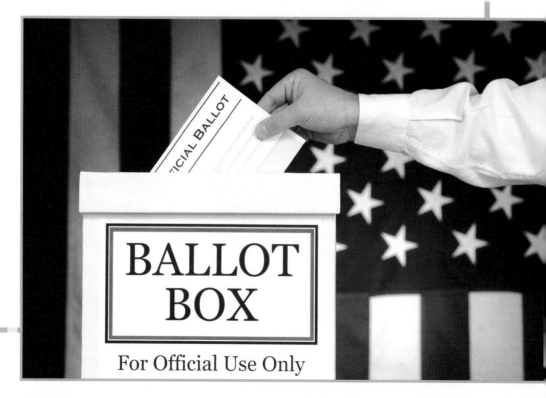

BALLOT BOX

For Official Use Only

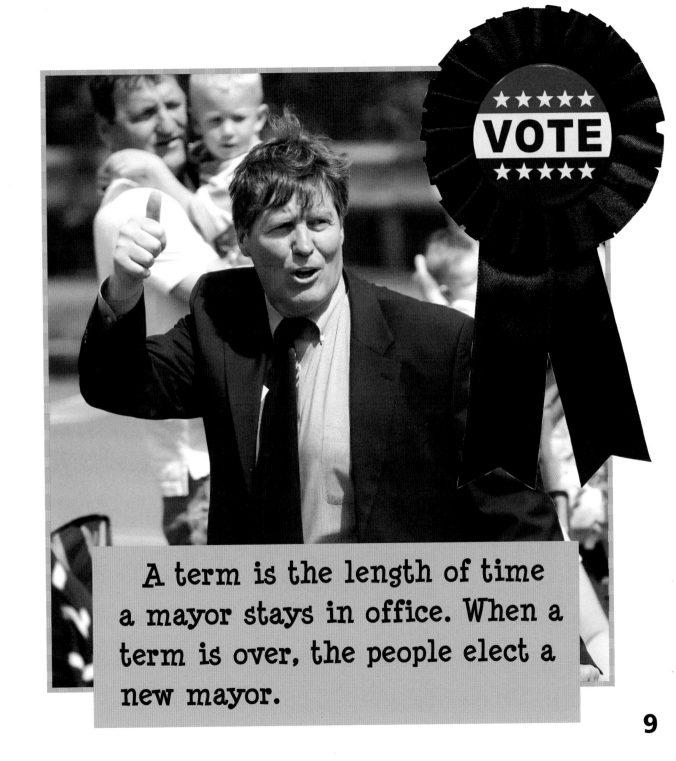

A term is the length of time a mayor stays in office. When a term is over, the people elect a new mayor.

City Council

Citizens elect **city council** members, too. The city council helps the mayor. Together, they make important decisions for the community.

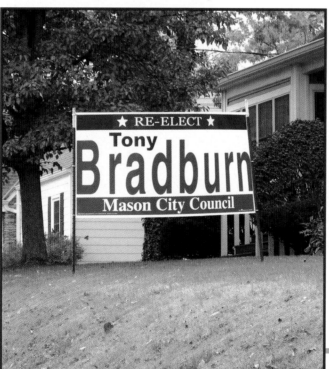

Signs let everyone know who is running for office.

A mayor and council members meet at city hall.

What Does a Mayor Do?

Mayors sometimes help create local laws. Laws protect the rights of community members. Laws help communities run smoothly.

A mayor signs a law for a special day for the U.S. Air Force.

Communities collect **taxes** to pay the government's bills. The mayor helps decide how the tax money is spent.

Community taxes help pay for new roads.

Taxes help support community police departments.

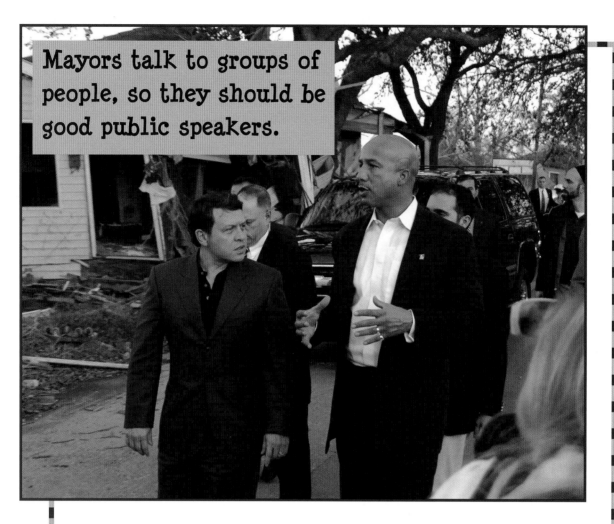

Mayors talk to groups of people, so they should be good public speakers.

Mayors attend city meetings, parades, and other important events. Mayors are the voice of the community.

Mayors take part in celebrations for new buildings.

Mayors lead communities of all sizes. A big city mayor might have different duties than a mayor of a small town. But no matter the size, a community needs leadership.

The mayor of New York City speaks to a crowd.

A Tough Job

Being a mayor is not easy. A mayor leads during good times, but must also be ready to take control during hard times.

Sometimes a mayor has to take charge
during an emergency.

A Better Place to Live

A mayor is important to a community. A mayor works hard to make a community a better place to live.

Be a good citizen and learn about your local leaders.

Glossary

citizens (SIT-I-zuhnz): people who live in a community

city council (SIT ee-KOUN-suhl): people chosen to help lead a commnunity

governments (GUHV-urn-muhnts): systems by which communities are controlled

taxes (TAKS-ez): money paid to support government

INDEX

FURTHER READING

Kishel, Ann-Marie. *What is Government*? Lerner Publications, 2007.

Silate, Jennifer. *Your Mayor*. Rosen Publishing Group, 2003.

Smalley, Carol. *State and Local Government*. Perfection Learning, 2005.

WEBSITES

http://bensguide.gpo.gov/
http://www.kids.gov/

ABOUT THE AUTHORS

David and Patricia Armentrout specialize in non-fiction children's books. They enjoy exploring different topics and have written about many subjects, including sports, animals, history, and people. David and Patricia love to spend their free time outdoors with their two boys and dog Max.